MW01119838

PENGUINS
FROM HEAD TO TAIL

By Emmett Martin

Gareth Stevens
PUBLISHING

Please visit our website, www.garethstevens.com. For a free color catalog of all our high-quality books, call toll free 1-800-542-2595 or fax 1-877-542-2596.

Library of Congress Cataloging-in-Publication Data

Names: Martin, Emmett, author.
Title: Penguins from head to tail / Emmett Martin.
Description: New York : Gareth Stevens Publishing, [2021] | Series: Animals from head to tail | Includes index.
Identifiers: LCCN 2019043398 | ISBN 9781538255285 (library binding) | ISBN 9781538255261 (paperback) | ISBN 9781538255278 (6 pack) | ISBN 9781538255292 (ebook)
Subjects: LCSH: Penguins–Juvenile literature.
Classification: LCC QL696.S473 M364 2021 | DDC 598.47–dc23
LC record available at https://lccn.loc.gov/2019043398

First Edition

Published in 2021 by
Gareth Stevens Publishing
111 East 14th Street, Suite 349
New York, NY 10003

Copyright © 2021 Gareth Stevens Publishing

Editor: Therese Shea
Designer: Laura Bowen

Photo credits: Cover, p. 1 (penguin) Natural Earth Imagery/Shutterstock.com; p. 5 Junko Kimura/ Staff/Getty Images News/Getty Images; p. 7 Martin Ruegner/Stone/Getty Images; p. 9 © Tim Davis/ Corbis/VCG/Corbis Documentary/Getty Images Plus/Getty Images; p. 11 James Hager/robertharding/ robertharding/Getty Images Plus/Getty Images; p. 13 fieldwork/Shutterstock.com; pp. 15, 24 (webbed) Gilles MARTIN/Contributor/Gamma-Rapho/Getty Images; p. 17 elmvilla/E+/Getty Images; p. 19 Education Images/ Contributor/Universal Images Group Editorial/Getty Images; pp. 21, 24 (chick) KeithSzafranski/E+/Getty Images; p. 23 Paul Souders/Stone/Getty Images.

Printed in the United States of America

Some of the images in this book illustrate individuals who are models. The depictions do not imply actual situations or events.

CPSIA compliance information: Batch #CS20GS: For further information contact Gareth Stevens, New York, New York at 1-800-542-2595.

Find us on

Contents

Penguins are birds.
They can't fly.

They walk on land.
They slide on ice and snow!

They swim!

Most are black and white.

They have short wings.
They have short legs.

They have webbed feet.

Feathers keep them warm.

They lay eggs.
They keep the eggs warm.

Chicks come out!

There are 18 kinds
of penguins.
The emperor penguin
is the biggest!

Words to Know

chick

webbed

Index

24